AF143856

BOOK ANALYSIS

By Cassandra Gibbons

On Beauty

BY ZADIE SMITH

ZADIE SMITH

ENGLISH NOVELIST AND ESSAYIST

- **Born in London in 1975.**
- **Notable works:**
  - *White Teeth* (2000), novel
  - *NW* (2012), novel
  - *Feel Free* (2018), essay collection

Zadie Smith is a British author who shot to fame at the tender age of 24 after her debut novel, *White Teeth*, was published to rave reviews and won a slew of awards. A string of critically acclaimed novels, short stories and essay collections followed, including her most recent novel, *Swing Time*, which was longlisted for the Man Booker Prize (her second nomination after *On Beauty* was shortlisted in 2005). She is also a tenured professor of Creative Writing at New York University.

Smith, who changed her name from Sadie to Zadie aged 14, grew up in Willesden before reading English Literature at Cambridge. Her novels tend to incorporate characters with similar life experiences to herself (for example, much of her fiction is set in north-west London and features characters of British-Jamaican heritage) although she has stated that her work is not explicitly autobiographical. She has been hailed as the literary face of multicultural Britain.

ON BEAUTY

AN HOMAGE TO E.M. FORSTER

- **Genre:** novel
- **Reference edition:** Smith, Z. (2005) *On Beauty*. London: Penguin Random House.
- **1st edition:** 2005
- **Themes:** race, class, religion, art, beauty, sex, relationships, politics

On Beauty is Smith's third novel and is loosely based on *Howards End* by E.M. Forster. Smith herself described the novel as an 'homage' to Forster, a writer to whose influence she considers herself indebted. The novel was well received by critics and won the 2006 Orange Prize for Fiction. It was also shortlisted for the Man Booker Prize in the year of its publication. The novel marked a return to form for Smith, whose second novel, *The Autograph Man,* had failed to win as many plaudits as her critically adored debut *White Teeth.*

On Beauty tells the story of two families, the Belseys and the Kippses, who come from opposite sides of the political and spiritual divide and whose lives gradually become more and more entwined. The Belseys are liberal atheists, headed by African American matriarch Kiki and her white British professor husband Howard, who are based in the fictitious university town of Wellington, near Boston. The Kippses are headed by conservative Trinidadian professor Monty Kipps, and are largely based in the UK, though Monty's work brings the family to Wellington. The novel explores the relationships between individual members of the families against the backdrop of a university town in the racially divided United States.

SUMMARY

TWO SUMMERS

The novel begins with a series of emails from Jerome Belsey describing his summer internship in London with Monty Kipps. The emails are addressed to his father, and though the reader is not privy to any replies from Howard, it is implied that they exist and are short and brusque. Jerome tells his father about how much he loves life with a family who share his Christian values, and how he has also fallen for Victoria Kipps, Monty's daughter, and is planning to propose to her. In his final, short email he tells his father that he was wrong to assume a relationship with Victoria, and that it is all over now.

Back in the United States, Howard is concerned to receive the email from Jerome detailing his plans to marry Monty Kipps' daughter. Howard and Monty are rival academics in the same field – Art History, with a speciality in Rembrandt – and Howard is sore from a recent article in which Monty humiliated him. Howard is going to London anyway, and so decides to leave early in order to see Jerome and convince him that getting married so young – in particular to the daughter of Howard's nemesis – is a bad idea. Kiki receives Jerome's final emails explaining that his relationship with Victoria is finished, but has no way of alerting Howard, who is already on his way to the airport, as he does not have a cell phone.

An embarrassing scene in London ensues. Howard is escorted to the Kippses' house by Michael, Monty's son, who is outraged to hear about a relationship between Jerome and Victoria. He tells Howard that Victoria is a virgin, and will stay that way until marriage due to the family's Christian beliefs. In fact, Victoria and Jerome have had sex once. Michael threatens Jerome upon return to the house but is told to leave him alone by Carlene Kipps, Monty's wife, who explains that there was a misunderstanding of feelings between Jerome and Victoria and that it is all settled now. Howard leaves with his son before seeing Monty.

The following summer, Jerome is still forlorn after his failed love affair with Victoria. Kiki and Howard's marriage is in trouble because Howard has had an affair. The couple and their three children (Jerome and his younger siblings, Zora and Levi) go together as a family to a Mozart concert. Despite the frostiness in their marriage, the Belseys manage a relatively convivial family atmosphere. They meet a young black man named Carl at the concert, who is from a much less privileged background than them and does his best to keep up with culture by attending free events like the Mozart concert – although his passion is actually rap music. Kiki invites Carl to her and Howard's anniversary party.

On the day of the party, Levi is happy to get out of helping with the preparations by going to his Saturday job at a record store. He is brusque with an old black woman who lives nearby and tries to engage him in conversation. Kiki realises that this must have been Mrs Kipps and, worried that her son was rude, goes around to invite her and her family to the party. While Carlene does not attend the party, the rest of the Kipps family does. Carl also shows up, but Howard rudely rebuffs him. Claire Malcolm, Howard's colleague with whom he had the affair (he told Kiki that it was a one night stand with an unknown woman), asks Howard to introduce her to Monty. Kiki notices the way Claire touches Howard and realises the truth. She decides not to make a scene at the party, but tells Howard that she will kill him if he ever comes near her again.

THE NEW SCHOOL YEAR

Zora begins her sophomore year of college determined to change herself. She takes particular care with her appearance and decides to go swimming in the mornings before class. She runs into Carl at the swimming pool and feels a deep sexual attraction to him. She is dismayed that she has not been accepted into Claire Malcolm's popular poetry class despite her high grades and published articles. She complains to the Dean and suggests that Claire has kept Zora out of the class deliberately because of her affair with Howard. Claire is outraged when she is effectively told to add Zora into her class, and maintains that Zora was not accepted because she has no talent for poetry. She bitterly relents when the Dean explains that Zora could create trouble if she is not accepted into the class.

Meanwhile, Howard is surprised to find Victoria Kipps in his class. Kiki becomes friends with Carlene Kipps, going over to her house with a pie and discussing art. Levi is outraged that he is expected to work Christmas day at his job, and tries to organise some sort of protest action amongst his co-workers. He notices that only his white colleagues show up to his impromptu meeting. His boss furiously tells Levi to not act like a "nigger" (p. 259); in other words, he knows that Levi affects his language and mannerisms in order to disguise his middle-class background, and he should not encourage his co-workers to risk their jobs. Unlike Levi, some of them actually need their income. Levi leaves his job, furious, and falls in with a crowd of Haitian street sellers.

Zora and Levi go to the Bus Stop – an entertainment venue that puts on poetry readings – together, but separate upon arrival. Zora is going as part of Claire's class, while Levi meets up with his new Haitian friends. They perform politicised spoken word poetry, much of it in French, with Levi acting as their 'hype man'. Zora is popular in her class but Claire is irritated to be sat near her. They go out together for a cigarette and Claire asks if they are ok. Zora quickly tells her that she does not see how Claire's affair with Howard should affect their student-teacher relationship. They go back inside to find Carl performing. He does incredibly well, and kisses Zora when he gets off the stage. Claire invites him to join their poetry class.

Claire asks Zora to argue in favour of Carl, and others, staying in the poetry class even though they are not full-time students at Wellington. Zora, who is enamoured of Carl, delightedly accepts the invitation: arguing in favour of something she believes in at a faculty meeting is a dream come true for her. Meanwhile, Levi becomes closer to his Haitian friends, and works part time with them selling items in the street. Howard is invited to a formal university dinner by Victoria Kipps, who has been flirting with him. Kiki's friendship with Carlene grows closer, and they go Christmas shopping together. Despite Kiki's protestations, Carlene plans on buying her new friend a gift.

THE DEATH OF CARLENE KIPPS

Over the Christmas break, when both the Belseys and the Kippses are in London, Carlene dies from a cancer that she had hidden from her family. The

Kippses are horrified to discover a handwritten note amongst Carlene's possessions leaving a very valuable painting to Kiki. They burn the note and decide to never mention it again. Nevertheless, the Belseys are invited to the funeral and go at Kiki's insistence, but Howard is overcome by feelings of death during the service and leaves. He visits his father, Harold, with whom he has a poor relationship due to Harold's racism. Howard gets drunk and then goes to the wake to find his family. The Belseys do not seem to be present, but while looking for them Howard ends up in Victoria's room, where she initiates sex.

After the Christmas break the university have a faculty meeting, in which both Howard and Zora give speeches in defence of liberal ideas. Howard argues that Monty should divulge the content of his provocatively titled lectures lest they include any homophobia. Howard's notion is refused point blank by Monty, and the rest of the faculty vote in favour of letting the lectures go ahead as planned. Zora, on the other hand, has great success when she gives her speech and manages to defer the decision on non-students (like Carl) being allowed to attend classes for one month: a significant victory. Victoria reminds Howard that he agreed to go to the university formal dinner with her, which he does, although he is loath to spend more time with her. When a glee club performs, Howard is unable to control his laughter and leaves, humiliating Victoria. He bonds with Kiki over the incident (she also finds glee clubs hilarious), but their marital problems remain unfixed.

Kiki has her liberal views challenged by Monty, who refuses to help one of Claire's other non-student students, Chantelle. Levi is further politicised by his Haitian friends. Claire asks a colleague to hire Carl as a hip-hop archivist, thus entitling him to attend classes. Zora is delighted and tries to hold his attention, but he is far more interested in Victoria. Howard goes to a hotel with Victoria but is put off by the way she speaks to the cleaner, and leaves. Victoria furiously breaks up with him, tells him to delete the explicit photos she sent him and drops out of his class. Howard is angry to see Kiki at one of Monty's lectures, although she claims to be simply listening to the other side of the debate.

Their argument becomes heated and they end up having sex, although Kiki is unsure about the future of their relationship.

Events come to a head at a frat party that is attended by all three Belsey children. Jerome and Zora get very drunk, and when Zora realises that Carl is kissing Victoria in a closet, she furiously drags him out and causes a scene. He thanks her for her help in keeping him in the poetry class but explains that he is not interested in her romantically or sexually. Zora, in her anger, calls Victoria a slut and demeans Carl. Carl hits back by telling Zora and Jerome that Victoria had sex with Howard, and also that Monty has been having sex with Chantelle. The next day, Zora is called into the university because a painting belonging to Monty has been stolen from the Black Studies Department. Kiki discovers the painting under Levi's bed – he had stolen it with the intention of selling it and redistributing the funds to poor Haitians. Jerome discovers a note on the back of it that reveals that Carlene meant for Kiki to inherit it. Zora confronts her father about Victoria and, when he cannot explain, tells her mother. A few months later, Kiki has moved out and Howard is about to give an important lecture on Rembrandt. His relationship with his three children is strained, and he struggles to adapt to domestic life while on sabbatical (Zora insists that he take some time away from work). His lecture does not go well, but Kiki attends and the two share a smile, with the implication being that there might be a future for them after all.

CHARACTER STUDY

HOWARD BELSEY

Howard Belsey is a white English professor of Art History who lives in the United States with his African American wife, Kiki, and their three transatlantic children. His marriage, and its deterioration due to his repeated infidelity, forms a significant part of the novel's plot. He first cheats on his wife with his colleague Claire, who is not considered to be as beautiful as Kiki, but who is much slimmer. He does so not out of particular affection for Claire, and deeply regrets the impact the affair has on his marriage. His affair with Victoria is more lust-driven, as she is not only very beautiful, but also young. Howard is portrayed as shallow in nature, and too focused on the aesthetic. He has fulfilling sex with his wife but still feels the need to point out her weight gain in the context of defending his indiscretions. Howard is portrayed as mean in other ways: for example, he does not tolerate any celebration of Christmas in his household despite the wishes of the rest of his family. Kiki complains that he forces his obsessions and resolutions on the rest of the family without their consent. By the end of the novel Howard is subdued, acting as the parental figure after Kiki moves out, and has to begin to win back his family's trust and affection.

KIKI BELSEY

Kiki Belsey is a nurse who has devoted her life to her husband and family. She is originally from Florida, and has followed Howard to England and back, uprooting her life according to his academic employment. She resents this when she realises that he has betrayed her not once, but twice, with conventionally better-looking women than her. Kiki strives to be a good mother, even though her relationships with her children are inconsistent. She is closer to her sons than her daughter, but struggles to communicate with all three of them at various points in the novel. Kiki is defined primarily by her kind, affectionate nature. She ignores the feud between her husband and Monty Kipps and strikes up a friendship with Carlene. Despite the Kippses' assumptions, she does not push Carlene to leave her the expensive painting, and she is careful to draw boundaries wherever necessary. She frets over her position as a privileged, middle-class black woman and is conflicted about hiring a Haitian cleaner for her house.

ZORA BELSEY

Zora is Howard and Kiki's ambitious, headstrong daughter and middle child. She does not have her mother's beauty, and although popular, has not had romantic success by the beginning of her second year at university. She is characterised by her determination and strong willpower. When she fails to get into Claire Malcolm's poetry class, she builds a strong case before presenting it to the Dean in a very articulate manner. She has an excellent understanding of university politics and uses this understanding to get herself into the class. It is unclear whether her efforts to keep Carl in the poetry class stem from her sexual desire for him, her liberal politics or the desire to debate and win over the faculty of the university at the highest level. It is quite possible that her drive is split between these three motivations. She is meticulous in her appearance, applying make-up with the greatest care, taking up swimming in order to maintain her figure, and choosing her outfits carefully (if not always stylishly). By the end of the novel, she seems to have reached the conclusion that beauty is not everything, having marvelled at how little time it takes to get ready when not obsessing over one's appearance. She thinks about what she could achieve in that time and seems to come to the conclusion that beauty is not necessary.

LEVI BELSEY

Levi is Howard and Kiki's youngest child, and acts as the moral compass of the novel, albeit a misguided one. Though not as academic as the rest of his family, he thinks about his blackness perhaps more than any of them. He compares his privileged situation with that of other young black men, and decides to mimic their lifestyles (including dress code, speech styles and mannerisms) in some sort of attempt at solidarity. He falls in with a group of Haitian workers and becomes politicised by them. In a botched attempt to redistribute wealth, he steals one of Monty's paintings from the Black Studies Department, a crime for which Carl, an under-privileged young black man, is almost blamed.

MONTY KIPPS

Monty Kipps is a conservative Art History professor, originally from Trinidad, who has settled in England and moves to America over the course of the novel. He is defined by his conservative views against affirmative action, sex outside marriage and gay marriage, the latter two of which he attributes to his Christian beliefs. He is a strong proponent of free speech, and declines Howard's demand that he share the content of his provocatively titled lecture series. He is a powerful speaker, and convinces the faculty to let his lectures go ahead. He is generally depicted through the perceptions of others, which results in a rather negative portrayal of his characteristics and personality. Kiki, for example, is suspicious of him and worries that he keeps Carlene in the house against her will. Howard is blinded by his political disagreement with the man and also, though he dare not mention it, his jealousy of Monty's achievements. Ultimately, Monty is shown to be a hypocrite. While preaching against sex outside marriage, he has been having an affair with Chantelle, a young woman who goes to his church, attends Claire's poetry class, and works as Monty's intern over the Christmas break during which Carlene dies. He is essentially blackmailed into accepting that discretionary students like Chantelle and Carl be allowed to study at the university.

VICTORIA KIPPS

Victoria is the daughter of Monty and Carlene Kipps. Like the rest of her family, she professes to adhere to strict Christian principles like chastity, but in reality she is sexually active. She has a brief sexual relationship with Jerome at the very start of the novel, but rebuffs him when he professes his love and suggests marriage. She seduces Howard at her mother's wake, telling him that "Jerome's lovely, but he's a *boy*, Howard. I need a man right now" (p. 429). When Howard finally ends his affair with her, she immediately begins sending explicit photos to Carl by email, and quickly initiates a sexual relationship with him. She is extremely intelligent, but places much of her self-worth in her not inconsiderable beauty. This ultimately does not bring her happiness.

CARL THOMAS

Carl is a young poet/rapper who meets the Belseys at a free Mozart concert. Kiki invites him to her anniversary party, which she suspects will be full of white people; she explicitly invites Carl so that there will be more guests of colour, and tells him so. Carl is hesitant to get involved with the family and later professes to regret it when Zora acts like she is sexually entitled to him because she has defended his right to study at Wellington as a discretionary student. Carl is not entirely blameless in his botched friendship with Zora, as he kisses her full on the mouth after performing at the Bus Stop. He ultimately values beauty more than loyalty, and is thrilled to begin a relationship with Victoria. Carl is essentially treated by the Belsey family as a class experiment: they use him as a pawn in testing their political theories, none more so than Zora (although she admittedly cares for Carl too).

ANALYSIS

LITERARY INFLUENCE AND INSPIRATION

Smith has stated explicitly that she found inspiration for the novel in E.M. Forster's *Howards End* (it is unlikely to be a coincidence that Howard Belsey shares the name of the eponymous house in Forster's novel). The plot of the novel is very loosely based on the events of *Howards End*, though obviously transposed to modern America. The openings of both novels mirror each other: *Howards End* begins with letters written by Helen Schlegel to her sister. *On Beauty* begins with emails written by Jerome to his father: the same form with a modern twist. Certain plot points from *On Beauty* can be found in *Howards End*. For example, Jerome and Victoria's short and doomed engagement mirrors that of Forster's Helen Schlegel and Paul Wilcox. Ruth Wilcox leaves the eponymous property to Margaret Schlegel in her will, which inspired Carlene's handwritten will bequeathing her valuable painting to Kiki.

More broadly, both novels tell the stories of two families with opposing views who find themselves gradually being drawn together. In *On Beauty,* the Belseys and the Kippses are linked at first by nothing more than a feud between their respective patriarchs. This connection deepens when Jerome interns for Monty, a decision that was possibly taken with the intention of needling his nemesis, Howard (Monty is proven elsewhere in the book to hire interns for non-professional reasons, like when he hires Chantelle, with whom he is having an affair). The entanglement of the two families grows ever closer as the Kippses move to the same town as the Belseys. This culminates in friendship between Carlene and Kiki and a sexual relationship between Victoria and both Jerome and Howard.

Smith also took inspiration from her own life when writing *On Beauty,* which, like many of her novels, contains details that coincide with her own life and work. She wrote part of *On Beauty* while a fellow at Harvard, and displays an intimate knowledge of university faculty politics. She even inserts herself into the novel in a small cameo, escaping the faculty meeting before Howard's speech, drawing attention to the pettiness of faculty politics:

"One lucky sod now escaped through the squeaky double-doors – a feckless novelist on a visiting fellowship – but she did not retire unobserved. Beady Liddy watched her go and made a note." (p. 437)

RACE

Race is perhaps the dominant theme in the novel. The novel's main characters are predominantly black, but each interacts with race in their own unique way, which culminates in a multi-faceted insight into what race is in America (and to a lesser extent in the UK) in the early 21st century. The tension surrounding race is underpinned by political tensions relating to the Haitian population, who have fled turmoil and strife in order to work low-paid, and sometimes illegal jobs, in the United States. Ideas about reparations for historical wrongs done to the black population are discussed, and memorably attempted with Levi's theft of Monty's valuable Haitian painting. The irony is that Levi, a privileged black teenager, is not immediately suspected, whereas Carl, a black man from a poorer background, becomes suspect number one despite his innocence. The idea of reparations in such a direct manner is shown to be simplistic when Kiki reveals that the painting was not stolen or defrauded from the Haitian population by Monty, but rather belonged to Carlene Kipps before she even married him.

The Belsey children, who have one white and one black parent, struggle in their own ways with their identity. Levi, who hides his middle-class upbringing by affecting certain speech patterns and mannerisms defined as 'street', is the obvious example. Given his privilege, his actions could almost be classed as 'cultural appropriation'. He is terrified at the prospect of being 'outed' as middle class, which his boss threatens to do. Despite his showy affectations, he is perhaps one of the most racially conscious characters, even if he goes about expressing his black culture in a counterproductive way. He finds himself thinking about how different his life as a young black man in America would be if he did not have the safety net of wealthy parents to fall back on. Levi acts as a moral conscience when he points out to Kiki that she only pays her Haitian cleaner Monique $4 an hour, something which has been gnawing at Kiki's sensibilities. Nevertheless, he is not immune to buying into certain clichés and stereotypes himself. When he comes across Carl in the university, he struggles to believe that his friend has found employment there, which offends Carl.

The female characters interact with race in a particularly interesting way, in part because of the way in which society views and values women. Black women in particular are often overly sexualised, and in *On Beauty* there are both examples of this sexualisation and also examples which contradict this stereotype. Kiki, for example, is sometimes vulgar in her language when discussing her sexual desire: "I see pretty boys every day of the week, and I think about their cocks, and what they would look like butt naked-" (p. 283). But in fact, it is her white husband, Howard, who is the more uncontrollably sexual of the two. Kiki is particularly hurt by Howard's decision to have an affair with a white woman who is much thinner than she is. She is presumably sensitive to the idea of people sticking with their own races for sexual and romantic relationships given the bigotry that is directed towards mixed-race couples (an example of which comes from Howard's father Harold, who implies that it is in Kiki's nature to be with a black man) and feels doubly betrayed by her husband: once for the act of adultery itself, and secondly, for seemingly acquiescing to the standard of same-race coupling.

Victoria, on the other hand, is an example of a young black woman who sexualises herself, partly in order to break free from her conservative Christian background, and partly to gain male gratification. Zora is the opposite of Victoria in looks: she is plainer and has less sex appeal, but by the end of the novel comes to see this as a blessing, as it frees her to focus on her true passions without the distraction that is male objectification.

> "For the first time in months, she got dressed without attention to anything else except the basic practical covering of her body. She didn't do her hair. No make-up. No contact lenses. No heels. How much time she saved! How much more she would get done in this new life!" (p. 567)

THE POLITICAL DIVIDE

On Beauty tackles lots of political issues that have become even more commonplace in popular discussion since the publication of the novel in 2005. Smith presents these issues in a balanced light, presenting arguments both for and against certain ideas with a politically-mixed group of characters. The novel is certainly sympathetic to the liberal sensibilities of Claire and Howard, by showing the benefits of educating less privileged people like Carl at Wellington. Nevertheless, the obstinacy and moral superiority of certain liberal characters, like Zora, for example, is at times exaggerated to the point of extreme irritation. Her desire to defend Carl's place in the poetry class smacks of selfishness: her views may be liberal, but her willingness to help Carl cannot be separated from her deep sexual attraction to him. When compared with Levi's friendship with Chouchou, Zora's motivations come to seem much less honourable than they first appear.

Monty's portrayal in the novel as a staunch conservative is interesting. Much less of the novel is presented from his perspective, and although in a way he dominates, as the enemy of Howard, his thoughts are notably absent from the novel on the whole. This is in contrast to his lecture series, which is given permission to go ahead without prior consultation of the content and without censorship. His complaint that his free speech is being curtailed does not stand up to scrutiny: his speech is not inhibited at all. He is, however, portrayed as a hypocrite. His preaching of Christian values, including a particular emphasis on no sex outside marriage, turns out to be only skin deep as he is having an affair with Chantelle, a discretionary student and his intern over the Christmas holiday period. His values do not stretch to his own personal behaviour, and in this he plays the archetypal role of the hypocritical conservative. Overall, due to Monty's hypocrisy and the possibility of Howard's redemption at the end of the novel, *On Beauty* leans slightly to the liberal side in drawing its conclusions.

FURTHER REFLECTION

SOME QUESTIONS TO THINK ABOUT...

- Discuss the role beauty plays in *On Beauty*.
- Does the novel make a case for or against affirmative action? Explain your answer.
- Both Howard and Monty have sex outside of marriage. Which of the two, in your opinion, is more hypocritical in doing so?
- Discuss the representation of Haiti in the novel.
- Can this novel be described as political fiction? Why/why not?
- To what end is music used in the novel?
- Make the case either for or against discretionary students. Use the text to back up your arguments.
- Compare *On Beauty* with another of Zadie Smith's novels you have read.

We want to hear from you!
Leave a comment on your online library
and share your favourite books on social media!

FURTHER READING

REFERENCE EDITION

- Smith, Z. (2005) *On Beauty*. London: Penguin Random House.

MORE FROM BRIGHTSUMMARIES.COM

- Reading guide – *NW* by Zadie Smith.
- Reading guide – *Swing Time* by Zadie Smith.
- Reading guide – *White Teeth* by Zadie Smith.

www.brightsummaries.com

Ebook EAN: 9782808019620

Paperback EAN: 9782808019637

Legal Deposit: D/2019/12603/148

Cover: © Primento

Digital conception by Primento, the digital partner of publishers.